MIDNIGHT EDITION

THE CROSS

And Snowflakes Mandala Patterns

Vol.2

Inspired Art Therapy, Flowers and Doodle Style

A Coloring Book for Adults

www.ingramcontent.com/pod-product-compliance
Lightning Source LLC
Chambersburg PA
CBHW051949280526
45789CB00009B/3226
* 9 7 8 1 5 4 0 8 8 7 8 8 7 *